Notes from the Camp Bunk

Notes from the Camp Bunk

A Guide for First-Time Campers from a Camper

— by Eden Martin —

ISBN: 978-1-938394-67-6

Library of Congress Catalog Number: 2021910916

published by:
Great Life Press
Rye, New Hampshire 03870
www.greatlifepress.com

Book design & layout: Grace Peirce

Cover art and illustrations by:
Pen at Hand, Inc.
www.morethanpaper.com

Contact the author
email: Eden@EastCoastSummerCamps.com

Contents

Acknowledgments

I would like to thank all the people who helped me in writing this guide. Special thanks to Michael Thompson Ph.D. for meeting with me and providing super helpful feedback. Also, thank you Liz Diggins for coordinating. Thank you to Ariel Nazryan for your expertise and hearing my voice. Thank you Debbie Volk and Derek Volk. Shout out to Liz Ganem's writing club at The Willows Community School. Thank you to Laurie Rinke and Tony Stein for the best summers of my life and for the feedback and contributions to this book.

Notes from the Camp Bunk

A Guide for First-Time Campers from a Camper

By Eden Martin

Introduction

I'm writing this book because I know some kids are nervous, or have some questions, about sleepaway camp (also called overnight camp) and there doesn't seem to be any helpful books for kids, or written by a kid.

In my case, I knew since I was little that I was going to go to camp. My mom went to camp when she was a kid and she always told me that I could go too, as soon as I was in the second grade. But I still had a lot of questions.

Here's a list of questions I had:

- What is camp like?
- Where will I sleep?
- How's the food?
- What kinds of activities do they have?
- Why do people like camp so much?
- What if I miss my family?

🌳 What if I get sick?

🌳 How can I remember everyone's name?

🌳 Are the bathrooms and showers clean?

🌳 Is everyone else going to know someone but me?

🌳 Will people think I'm weird if I bring a stuffed animal?

🌳 Who's going to do the laundry?

🌳 What is Visiting Day?

🌳 Will I miss screen time?

🌳 What if I'm shy?

🌳 Most important: Who's going to make my ponytail in the mornings? (This really was a big concern of mine.)

History

A little history about sleepaway camp:
I found it interesting that people have
been going to camp since the late 1800s.
(It's an American tradition.) Back then, most
camps were either all girls or all boys and
they would go for 8-10 weeks (the whole
summer). The kids would take trains to get
to camp. These days there are still all-girls
and all-boys camps, but there are also coed
camps. You can choose to stay for the whole
summer or just for a few weeks. Most kids
take buses, cars, or planes to get to camp.

According to the American Camp
Association, about 11 million kids go to camp

each summer. Many camps are close to 100 years old. The camp I go to is about to turn 75 years old as I'm writing this book. So for 75 years, kids have been spending summers at my camp. Knowing that has made me feel part of something big!

I've also learned that in some regions of the country, it's really common for kids to go to camp and in others it's not. I happen to live in a city where sleepaway camp is not as common. Only a small number of my local friends go to overnight camp. Some of you may live where almost everyone in your class is going to a sleepaway camp.

What's so great about camp?

First, camps have so many different activities — ones that you may never have done before you went to camp. One of those for me was lacrosse. I'm a pretty sporty kid, so I go to a camp that has lots of athletics. They have tennis, basketball, golf, hockey, gymnastics, gaga, soccer, volleyball, and many more sports. Most camps, including mine, have lots of other activities too, like arts and crafts, woodworking, theater, dance, horseback riding, sailing, boating, water skiing, cooking, circus arts, ropes courses, mountain biking, hiking, and more. Your camp may have different activities.

No matter which activities you are doing at camp, one of the cool things is that your parents aren't there watching you. It's just you and your camp friends having fun.

I don't know about you, but I don't have a lake in my backyard! Camps are often really beautiful and in nature. It feels really peaceful being there.

Keep in mind: Camp isn't just about one summer, it's about lots of them. Most campers go back to the same camp each summer through high school. And now you get a whole other friend group in addition to all of your friends from school!

One of the truly best things about camp is that you get to be yourself no matter what. Living with people allows you to really get to know them and them to really get to know you. So you can get unbelievably close throughout the summer.

Life-lasting friends also means life-lasting memories, like inside jokes. You're probably going to catch yourself thinking about an inside joke between you and your camp friends years after it happened.

I have found myself lying on the floor a lot at camp because I was laughing so much.

What else makes camp so great? Between us, it feels really good and you feel proud of yourself when you get home because you've learned to do new stuff, made new friends, and survived without your parents.

Who is going to take care of me at camp?

Owners, directors, and head staff are the adults of the camp who supervise everybody. The directors at camp are usually the age of your parents, but they are a lot more fun than parents (even if they are one).

Head staff are people that you can talk to if something is bothering you, and they also run some of the activities, make the schedule for each group, help with some of the special events, and make sure that everybody is happy! The directors at camp are sometimes the owners of the camp, but not always. Camp directors are usually planning camp throughout the year. So they make sure that everything is going to be really fun. Overall the owners, directors, and senior/head staff are really cool people.

I asked Camp Owner Laurie Rinke what she thought was most important for new campers to know about camp owners, directors, and senior staff. This is what she said:

> "The job of camp directors/owners and camp counselors is to help make campers feel comfortable, make friends, do great activities, and have fun! Camp is made to help campers be their best selves, grow as a person, and learn things/make memories that will last a lifetime!"

Counselors

Along with the head staff, a wonderful part of camp is the counselors. Counselors are the people who supervise the kids at camp. Counselors are really nice and they're young (around 19 and 20 years old), so they're really fun! A lot of camp counselors come from different countries like Ireland, Australia, and England, as well as the United States. Sometimes their use of the English language is different than ours in the U.S. I now know what they mean when they say, "Use your torch to find your jumper." (Use your flashlight to find your sweatshirt.)

I think this chapter is important because in my first year going to camp I had no idea what the counselors would be like (and they were a lot better than I thought they were going to be). They are less strict than parents and they remember what it's like to be a kid.

The directors take a lot of time to think about which counselors would be the most fun, nice, funny, cool, and epic! Some of my favorite memories from camp involve times with my counselors.

Once I was coming back from the health center/infirmary at night, and I was getting a piggyback ride on my counselor's back and she thought that she saw something move near the plants — so then she got really close to the plants and we both looked and made eye contact with a skunk! We ran off laughing with me holding on super tight and we talked about that story the whole summer!

Why you might feel nervous about sleepaway camp

Some of you who are reading this book might be going to camp for just one week, or as many as two, three, four, or seven weeks. Keep in mind that it's normal for it to take a few days to get used to camp life. It could even take a week or two to really feel comfortable the first summer. It's different for everybody. Once you get used to the daily routines, you're going to want to have as much of camp left as possible.

One cool thing about staying at camp for a few weeks is that you get to learn new things and have time to get good at them. My first year of camp, I tried water skiing for the first time and splash! I fell right on my face. I didn't even stay up for one second, but now I can stay up for quite a few minutes and ski around the lake. This is because I was at camp for many weeks and got to practice many times. If you don't do so well when it's your first time doing an activity, don't worry because you can just practice it again and again over your stay at camp.

In my opinion, it's nice to spend a longer time with your camp friends (and trust me, it goes by too quickly). You really get to know each other and get really close.

Will my parents be okay without me?

It also seems that some kids are scared to go to camp because they think their parents are scared. You might be wondering if your parents will be okay without you. First of all, parents are just going to be doing that same boring stuff they always do when you are at home. They'll go to work and the grocery store and they'll have dinner. They may read some books or see some of their other adult friends. They will also be taking care of your pets and making sure no one moves your stuff while you are gone. My point is that they are not doing anything too fun, but they will be fine.

By the way, if they weren't okay with you going to camp, you probably wouldn't be reading this book.

What if I don't know anybody there?

You also might worry that you aren't going to know any of the people there. My parents have always said that I'm a slow-to-warm kid, which I guess means that I'm not that good at starting conversations. When I was first going to camp I was scared of the people there because I thought it was going to be awkward. And let me tell you that it is definitely not as awkward as you think it's going to be! At first, it might not be like talking to your best friend, but eventually it will be.

It's okay to be nervous about making friends! I have met some people at camp who were really shy and we still got super close once we both got used to camp. By our second summer together, we felt closer to each other than to some people that we have known our whole lives!

You just have to remember to be yourself. A few of my camp friends and I got close pretty fast and it took a couple of summers to get close with some of the others. But I promise you that whether it takes two hours or two summers you will be close with pretty much everyone in your group.

Will I miss screen time?

At first, the thought of life without screens might seem a little crazy! But having no screens at camp isn't at all like at home when you're really bored and you have nothing to do. At camp people are having so much fun that you won't even think about TV, phones, or video games even a little bit!

When I found out that there weren't going to be any screens at camp I thought that just the idea of it was insane! But I ended up being really happy that there weren't any screens at camp because that would have ruined it!

I'm sure that you have watched TV for a long time before, or binge-watched a show — well, imagine going to camp with all of your electronics. You probably wouldn't even be tempted to talk to anyone. And one of the best parts of camp is camp friends. By the way, just between us, camps usually do show a movie or two throughout the summer, especially if it is raining really hard.

It might take a little while to get used to it, but when you come home from camp it feels really good to know that you survived that long without screens. You might even be surprised that you didn't miss them as much as you had thought you would.

What if I get sick or take medication?

Don't worry, but it does happen sometimes. All sleepaway camps have something called the health center or the infirmary, and there are nurses and doctors. It kind of feels like going to the doctor's office at home. Sometimes if you have a fever you may have to sleep there overnight, but they have beds and air conditioning there and some have a TV (but don't tell anyone I told you that). And sometimes you get good stuff from being sick — once I had a stomach ache and they gave me Gatorade and ginger ale. But still, don't try to be sick.

Don't worry if you take medications because you're not going to be the only person there who takes medications in your group. A counselor will take you to the health center or infirmary, and you can take your medicine there. I take medicine at night so when I first got to camp I was really nervous that I was going to be the only one who took nighttime meds. But this turned out not to be true at all. A few of the kids took allergy medication, vitamins, melatonin, or growth hormone. Only the nurses know what medication you take, unless you choose to tell your friends. You can go to the health center anytime, even if you just have a headache or stomach ache.

Where will I sleep?

Most camps have cabins or bunks.
From the outside they look like mini houses.
Different camps call them different names
but they usually refer to them as cabins or
bunks (they are the same thing). At some
camps, campers sleep in a dorm, which
is more of a room, and at others, campers
sleep in tents. The bunks are likely to have a
name or a number. They may be named after
colleges, trees, mountains, or plants!

The interior of a cabin or bunk usually
has beds and cubbies.

You might be asking, where do I put my stuff? Well here's the answer: You usually have cubbies to put your clothes in, and they should either be next to your bed or in the back of the place you're staying in (unless you sleep in a tent).

There should also be cubbies for your books and games. And you could put your sports equipment under your bed.

Bathrooms and showers

Some showers are in the bunk, and if there aren't any showers in the bunk, then you probably have a shower house. A shower house is basically what it sounds like. It's a bunk full of showers. Either way you get privacy. You get to bring your own soap, shampoo, and towel from home. I also like to bring shower shoes and a shower caddy. Shower shoes are flip-flops (that sometimes have holes in them but not always) and a shower caddy is like a waterproof bag or bin meant for you to put your toiletries in.

When it was my first shower I had no idea how the system worked but it turned out that it was just like any other shower that you would have at home.

The bathrooms are also private at camp. They usually have one to three stalls or doors with toilets in each bunk, and there's usually a sink. There are also a lot of bathrooms scattered all over camp, so you don't have to worry about that.

In conclusion you get a lot of privacy in the showers and bathrooms.

A day in the life of a camper

Waking up at camp may be a little different from how you get woken up at home. Some camps play a traditional "reveille" on a trumpet or a recording of one. This is very traditional, going back to when camps first started, but most camps no longer do this. Many camps will play music or make an announcement on a P.A.

system when it is time to get up, or you may go to a camp where the counselors in your bunk wake you up. Once you are up, you go to breakfast with your cabin mates. It's not uncommon for people at camp to go to breakfast in their pajamas!

After breakfast you will usually go back to the place where you sleep and clean it for a prize. Sometimes you may wake up and clean up first and then have breakfast. After that, at many camps you go to a gathering that people either call "cove" or "lineup." Sometimes they raise the flag there, but not always, and they also make announcements. For example, they might say who won the prize for the cleanest bunk or announce an addition to the day's schedule.

Then it's time to do a few activities. You may have two or three activity periods before lunch. At some camps you do your activities with your bunkmates and at some camps you may do them with other kids at camp who are interested in the same activity.

Then it might be time for lunch. After lunch there is something called "rest hour" which is when you get to just chill for an hour, and that's a good time to play with your bunk junk (I will explain what bunk junk is in a later chapter). It's also a time to write letters to your family and friends.

After rest hour, there are some more activity periods. You might have something called canteen which is sometimes in the afternoon or evening. Canteen can be in its own building and is basically a snack that a camper chooses, like chips, gummy bears, popcorn, fruit rollups, and more!

At some point during the day there's swim. I've written more about spending time in the water, below. In the late afternoon, after afternoon activities are done and either before or after dinner, there may be evening cove or lineup.

Then there is dinner. You will probably shower either before or after dinner. After that you could have evening activity, which is a fun game or a performance in the evening. After that you might have a little snack or canteen.

Then it's flashlight time, which is when you can read or listen to music (with your air pods, headphones, or earphones), and then you go to bed.

Water

Most camps have something called a deep water test. The deep water test is a test to make sure campers are safe to go in the deep part of the lake or pool. How the deep water test works is that you just do a certain number of laps. If you have a lake at your camp then you would probably do the deep water test in there, but if you don't have a lake at your camp then you would do the test in the pool.

At my camp for the deep water test we have to swim two laps of breaststroke, two laps of backstroke, and two laps of front crawl/freestyle. I suggest practicing swimming at home, before you go to camp. If you don't know how to swim yet, do not worry. You'll get to do swim lessons at camp.

By the way, if you don't want to take the test, it just means you will need to swim in the shallow end until you pass. And if you don't make it the first time you do the deep water test then you can always try again throughout the summer, until you make it!

When you pass the deep water test then you can participate in water sports like sailing, water skiing, kayaking, and a lake swim (where you attempt to swim across the lake).

Most camps have swim lessons. Usually the swim lessons have different levels. The swim lessons at camp are better than if you were to do them at home because you are with all of your camp friends.

There are lifeguards at all camps, so all campers are safe in the water. For added safety, a buddy system may also be used at camp. No one swims alone at camp, not even just to play on the giant inflatable water toys some camps have. (They are super cool, by the way.) Overall, swimming at camp is really safe and fun!

Rainy days

Rainy days are different, but fun. Remember, camp staff always keeps everyone safe, so if there is lightning, you will probably stay inside and you might watch a movie, play dodgeball, or have bunk time. You also might have different food, like a hot chocolate or a brownie and stuff like that! But if there isn't any lightning or it's not raining hard, then you will probably still have whatever it says on the schedule. But don't be sad if it's a rainy day because it's still really fun!

Special days and events

The events at camp are really fun! I made a list of some events that you might have at camp:

Carnival

At carnival there are games, rides, and food. Some of the food might be chicken, pizza, cheeseburgers, donuts, cotton candy, snow cones, ice cream, or more! At some camps, each cabin gets to create and run their own booth or game. Examples of booths may be: the marriage booth, guess how many jelly beans are in the jar, ring toss, and throw a wet sponge at your favorite counselor. You get to take turns running your own booth and going around to the other groups' booths. My favorite memory from carival is beating Sami, who is a much older camper than me, at a watermelon eating contest. And sometimes there can be themes to the carnival — at my camp the theme is usually superheroes.

The Fourth of July

If you are going to be at camp for the Fourth of July then you are probably going to celebrate it there! You might have fireworks and special food! I suggest bringing some red, white, and blue clothing if you will be at camp for the celebration.

Hoedown

You might have something called hoedown at camp. Hoedown is kind of like a cowboy-themed party. You basically just dance and sing the whole time, but they will teach you the dances and songs beforehand. (The dances and songs aren't hard. It's kind of like the dance from Row, Row, Row, Your

Boat.) And I also suggest you bring cowboy-themed clothes for it.

Birthdays

B-days at camp are really fun because you get to celebrate with all of your camp friends! When it's someone's birthday in your group you get cake, and when it's your birthday you might get an extra phone call, favorite activities, and more! Another reason why it's really fun to have your birthday at camp is that you might get two birthdays instead of one, because you can celebrate with your parents either before or after camp, and also with all of your camp friends at camp!

Themed days

There are also a lot of themed days at camp. The day has to do with a theme, and you might dress up. They can be funky hat day, winter day, superhero day, be your camp friend day, and more! But they are all really fun! And don't worry if you don't have any clothing that has to do with the theme, because you can always borrow from a friend, and the themes are usually simple.

Campfires

The campfires at camp are fun! The stuff that you might do at a campfire is sing camp songs, read a book, do cheers, play games, and make and eat s'mores! It's also really cozy. But if you are worried that you're going to get some of your s'more on your clothes then I recommend that you wear something that you don't care about. So if you're worried about that then make sure that you pack at least one set of clothes especially for those types of events!

Trips

People go on trips at camp. Some common trips you might take are mini-golf, bowling, or to a water park. You might go hiking, you might go to the beach, some of the older kids at camp go on overnight trips to nearby cities. And if you go to an amusement park and you don't like rides at all then you don't have to go on any rides, and you can just explore or buy stuff at either a gift shop or store.

Intercamp games

There is also something called an intercamp game, which is when you play other camps in sports. Like when your school team plays against another school. Sometimes there are tournaments when a few different camps play each other. Sometimes intercamps and tournaments are played at your own camp and sometimes you take a bus to another camp.

Color War/Tribal/Olympics

At some camps there is something that is usually called "Color War," or "Olympics," or "Tribal," though they mean the same thing. Color War is when the camp splits up into teams (usually two teams) and the teams compete in sports, games, and even singing. This usually takes place over several days. The team who earns the most points wins. The teams wear different team colors and it is fun to wear the color of your team. You can even bring a green wig or a big blue hat for example. Usually the color war team leaders are older campers at camp and they are all really nice and have a lot of team spirit.

What about food?

Just like at home, sometimes you like the food and sometimes you don't, but the good thing about camp food is that there are a lot of choices. At some camps there are waiters (who used to be campers when they were younger), at others there's either a buffet where you actually go up and get the food right away yourself, or sometimes the counselors bring the food to the table. And don't be freaked out if they call the fruit punch "bug juice." It isn't really made out of bugs.

And mealtime isn't just about the food. It's a time where sometimes the campers do fun cheers, talk, and play games.

All camps have policies for allergies. Some camps are even nut-free. If you're allergic to the stuff they have, they will give you food that you're not allergic to. And if

you don't know whether you're allergic to
the food, then ask the kitchen staff if the
item has whatever you're allergic to in it.
For example I'm allergic to bananas and
sometimes there are muffins — so I just
double check with the kitchen staff to make
sure that the muffins don't have bananas in
them, and when they do, the kitchen staff
gives me something else that's good and
sweet like a muffin.

Keeping in touch and Visiting Day

Part of camp is keeping in touch with your parents. So make sure that you bring a lot of stationery, envelopes, and stamps so that you can write your family and friends letters. It can be very helpful to put the address and stamp on the envelopes while you are still at home. I usually bring lots of envelopes addressed to my parents and then a few addressed to my grandparents and my friends. For your first summer, I recommend bringing fill-in-the-blank stationery, which is when the stationery begins the sentence and you finish it!

There's a sample one on the next page:

Date: _____

To:_____

Camp is: _____

The food is: _____

I am having: _____

Today we did: _____

Tomorrow we are going to: _____

_____

You won't believe that I:_____

_____

My counselor is: _____

How is? _____

From: _____

    Every summer my first letter home says who's in my bunk and I even draw a picture of where the kids in my bunk sleep.

    By the way, another reason it's important to bring stationery is that at some camps people write "bus notes," which is when people write you a letter at the end of the summer with their contact information (so you can keep in touch during the winter) and a few things that they enjoyed about you!

Visiting Day

Your camp might have something called "Visiting Day," but not all camps have Visiting Day because it depends on how long your camp is. Visiting Day is when your parents come to your camp for one day and get to see you! They can bring food, toys, candy, supplies, and more (but not a pet)! You can't keep all of the stuff, but you can keep everything that's allowed at camp!

When they get there, you can give your parents a tour of your camp and you can do activities with them. You can swim, play basketball, show them your art projects, and basically do anything. And some camps let you go off campus, but not all camps. Usually, when the parents leave, the camp plans a really fun activity. At my camp the whole camp has a candy party, then we have a camp Halloween!

While it's great to see your parents, it can also be really sad to say goodbye to them at the end of the day. But don't worry because your friends and camp counselors will be there to cheer you up, give you a hug, and quickly get you back to the camp fun.

What if I get homesick?

"Homesick" basically means you miss home, your parents, and/or your pets. If you get homesick it's okay. It's normal to feel this way at first. Pretty much everybody feels a little homesick at times, especially the first summer away. It is not a bad thing to miss home.

Remember that head staff, counselors, and friends are there to help you. They are prepared to help you with homesickness. Nobody is going to make fun of you or think that you're weird because you miss home. Whenever one of my camp friends was sad and missing home, there was always a counselor there to help.

When one of my friends was feeling homesick it was at the very beginning of camp. I went to sit with her and we talked about all of the cool stuff coming up and how we were going to have a blast. She started to feel a little better so we went to play basketball and it was me and her vs. two other kids from my bunk and we won, which made her think about how the summer is going to be really fun once she gets more used to camp.

There was a different time when someone else from my bunk was super homesick so the first thing she did was tell a counselor and the counselor talked to her and told her that she knows the group leader really well and that she would definitely make her feel better. Both my friend and our counselor went to the group leader and they talked about how, once the first few days pass, it's going to be much better and how her phone call with her parents is in a couple of days and how she's sure that her dog is happy that she's going to have an awesome time at camp. She began to feel much better after that.

If you get homesick a tip is just to think about some good times at camp or about how, if you never went to camp, you would never have met any of your camp friends!

You also might be wondering what to do if you miss your dog or pet. Well, I have a few answers for that question! Before camp I asked my parents to send me my dog's paw prints in the mail. They also sent me a bunch of photos of him which helped too. I taped the photos up on the wall by my bed.

You can also do stuff that will help you when you're homesick before you even get to camp. I have made a list of some ideas to make it easier when you get homesick:

- 🌲 Make sure that you look at a lot of videos and pictures of the camp that you are going to, so you can picture yourself there.

- 🌲 You can also read all about your camp. Like the schedule, the menu, and more, so that you know what to expect.

- 🌲 You can practice spending a few nights away from home with relatives or friends. (Before I went to camp I went on an overnight field trip with my class.)

- 🌲 Bring something special from home that you wouldn't be too upset to lose. You can bring something special from home like a pair of your favorite pajamas. You can also bring some fidgets. Let's say that you get a little bit stressed — then you could play with a stress ball or something.

- 🌲 Ask for a special request. You might be wondering what I mean by a special request? Well, I mean that you could ask your parents or friends to send you something cool. I wrote a list of some stuff I wanted my parents to bring for Visiting Day.

If you're homesick you can always talk to a camp friend or a counselor about it (or even the camp director) because they will probably make you feel better.

You shouldn't be embarrassed if you get homesick!

I asked camp owner, Laurie Rinke, what she thinks is important for a first time camper to know about homesickness and this is what she said:

"Even though most campers and staff feel a little nervous before camp starts or when they first get to camp, camps and camp staff are really good and helping campers feel comfortable quickly and start having fun right away. That helps campers get over their initial nerves and start to adjust to the fun of camp. Once you are comfortable, you will have fun with friends, participate in activities you love, try new things, and want to be part of the entire camp experience. I have never seen a camper get more nervous or homesick over the length of time of camp! It is always the start to camp that can be a bit harder, because it's new, but your friends and counselors will help you feel comfortable and then you will want the full length of time at your camp to be with your friends and enjoy all the many awesome activities."

What if I want to go home?

You might be wondering what you're going to do if you want to go home. The thing about homesickness is that it comes and goes, meaning that sometimes you will feel homesick and sometimes you won't feel homesick. I have heard of a lot of people who were feeling homesick and wanted to go home but ended up being really happy that they didn't — when it was the last day of camp they were really sad because they didn't want to leave camp.

When someone is feeling like they want to go home, we talk about all of the awesome things at camp and remind them that they will see their parents soon — and even the people who are really scared about camp end up having a good time.

Stuff to pack

I'm writing this chapter because there's a lot of stuff you might need. Every camp will have its own packing list.

Here is a sample packing list:

_____ 10 t-shirts

_____ 3 long sleeved t-shirts

_____ 8-10 pairs of shorts

_____ 2 sweatshirts

_____ 2-3 pairs long pants (jeans or sweats)

_____ 2 hats

_____ 12 pairs of socks

_____ 12 pairs of underwear

_____ 2 pairs of sneakers

_____ 1 pair of field cleats

_____ 1 pair of flip-flops or crocs

_____ 1 pair of hiking boots

_____ 3-4 swimsuits

_____ 2 sets of comfortable sleepwear

_____ 2 blankets

_____ 2 twin-size sheet sets

_____ 1 pillow

_____ 5 standard size beach towels

_____ 1 raincoat

_____ 1 fleece or warm jacket

_____ 1 sleeping bag with stuff sack

_____ 2 soft trunks

_____ 1 pair of shin guards

_____ 1 tennis racquet

_____ 1 flashlight with extra batteries

_____ 2 water bottles

_____ 4 sets of stationery and stamps

_____ 2 disposable cameras (or an inexpensive camera)

_____ toothbrush and toothpaste

_____ hair brush (or wide-toothed comb)

_____ shampoo

_____ sunscreen & lip balm

_____ extra pair of eyeglasses

There's also some stuff you might want to bring that won't be on a packing list:

- 🦉 a clipboard for your stationery
- 🦉 stuff for Color War/Tribal
- 🦉 stuffed animal

♧ decorative pillow

♧ stuff for your wall (small poster or pictures)

♧ books

♧ games (but not electronic games)

♧ battery-operated fans

♧ plain shirt, plain pillowcase, or autograph pillow

♧ Crazy Creek Chair (makes sitting on the ground comfy)

♧ an egg crate

♧ a laundry bag

♧ "bunk junk"

♧ Bunk junk is stuff like…

- Mad Libs
- deck of cards
- stress balls
- cat's cradle string
- Rubik's Cube
- jacks
- mini balls
- Uno

And I would also bring a box for your bunk junk.

Trunks

A trunk is something that you put a lot of your stuff in to bring to camp. It is usually sent to camp before you get there, but not always. In some cases it will already be there and unpacked when you get there, and it might be on your bed.

You're probably wondering what goes in your backpack and what should go in your trunk so here is a list of some stuff that definitely should go in your trunk:

- 🌲 bedding
- 🌲 toiletries
- 🌲 clothes
- 🌲 sports equipment
- 🌲 stationery (including a clipboard, envelopes, and stamps)

But the rest of the stuff you should bring should be on your packing list.

It's really important that you put your name on everything, like clothes and sports equipment! Laundry at camp is usually once a week. You won't have to wash it yourself, but you will probably help sort it and that's when the name tags come in handy.

The Camp Bus

You might not know how you're going to get to camp yet. Some campers arrive by plane, car, or bus. It's really fun to go by bus, because then you can meet people on the way to camp. The bus ride goes by really fast because everyone's having a lot of fun with their camp friends, or getting to know someone who's going to be in their bunk or group.

On my first bus ride I didn't know who I was going to sit with because the people that I met when we were getting on the bus were already sitting with someone. So then I asked a new friend if we could sit together at some point in the bus ride (because she was already sitting with her siblings) and she said yes, so about five minutes later she came to sit with me and even introduced me to someone else who was going to be in our group. But the staff there make sure that you're sitting with someone, usually someone your age.

Tips

Even though some of these tips are weird, they still work!

♤ If you have Visiting Day and two phone calls, make sure that one of them is before Visiting Day and one of them is after Visiting Day, because you're going to want to tell your parents what you want for Visiting Day, like your favorite food and just stuff that you want. And it's just good to have your phone calls spread out. Generally they don't allow phone calls the first week of camp, so don't be suprised by that. While phone calls are nice to talk to you parents they might make you a little bit sad. But don't worry because your counselors and friends will be there to cheer you up and get you back to the fun.

🍀 When you don't like an activity, just think about how you are going to do your favorite activity soon, or how you will be able to have some free time with your friends later. But it's still really important to appreciate the moment and just try to have fun!

🍀 You should bring a few clothes that you don't care about because there are some messy activities.

🍀 You shouldn't bring anything that would make you really sad to lose. But let's say that you have a stuffed animal that you really like, and you can't sleep without it? I would just bring it, because you're going to want to have a good sleep because of all of the activities. And it's just going to be on your bed the whole time.

🍀 If it is your first summer at camp, you don't have to wait for your bunkmates to talk to you first. You'll be fine just introducing yourself. Everyone at camp remembers what it was like their first summer and they are all going to be super friendly.

🍀 If you happen to be going to camp in

a different state than where you live, do not worry. It turns out that it is really fun to have friends who live in a variety of places.

🌲 I suggest that when it's really close to camp you be more careful because it's not fun being injured at camp. A couple of years ago I got stitches on my hip and I got them out right before camp, but I was really lucky because if I had gotten just one more stitch I would have had to miss a lot of activities. (But if you are reading this book really close to camp and you are injured then don't worry and just really rest it!)

🌲 It can be a nice experience to go to camp without any school friends. No one knows you or remembers the dumb thing you did in kindergarten. You just get to be yourself. You also don't have to worry about if the friend you came with is enjoying camp or if you are making the same friends. Sometimes it can become awkward. It's actually refreshing to be with a different group of people.

🍄 You might be wondering how in the world you are going to remember everyone's name? Here's a list of tips to help you remember everyone's name.

- Try not to get stressed about remembering everyone's name!
- Play the name game.
- Think of people that you know at home who have the same name or a name that sounds like the name of the person you are trying to remember.
- Try to repeat their name multiple times.
- Try to remember that it's ok to ask them their name a lot because they are probably going to do that too.
- If you're having a lot of trouble remembering everybody's name at once then just start with remembering one name at a time.

I also asked my camp friends for tips they would give to new campers. Here are their answers:

"Establish yourself quickly and always be nice and try hard." —Izzy T.

"Don't be afraid to try new things and be yourself." —Stevie Z.

"Don't be afraid to be you, because everyone there will accept that you are unique." —Lauren G.

Questions and answers

Right now I'm going to answer some questions about camp. So here's a list of some stuff that you might want to know.

Question: Will people think I'm weird if I bring a stuffed animal?
Answer: No, because everyone else is probably going to bring a stuffed animal too.

Question: What if I get lost?
Answer: you never have to worry about getting lost. You are never anywhere without supervision. And you will never have to worry about finding anything by yourself.

Question: What if I hate all of the activities?
Answer: First of all, you're not going to hate all of the activities because there are so many, and because you've chosen a camp with activities that you know you'll like. And if you do hate an activity, just try to have fun with it!

Question: Will everybody know somebody except for me?
Answer: The answer is no. Usually most campers go to camp not knowing anyone ahead of time. During the first few days of

camp, the counselors help with everybody getting to know each other.

Have a great summer!

I asked some of my friends what they like best about camp. Here are some of their answers:

"I love camp because we get to make new friends and have the times of our lives for seven weeks. Also, I love camp because there are so many different activities and people to connect with." — Izzy T.

"All the memories we have and all the new friends I met because of camp." —Summer S.

"Meeting new people that become life long friends and having experiences I won't ever forget." —Carrington A.

We've come to the end of the book! Remember that it is normal for it to take a while to get used to camp at first. Whether it takes you just one day or a few days to get used to being there doesn't matter. Camp is still a really fun place and you will have the most awesome time.

So just remember all of the stuff you just read and you will know what to expect at camp. When you walk into your bunk for the first time you will know what is going on. Have fun!

By the way, my counselor, Emily, did my ponytail at camp!

About the Author

Eden Martin is a middle school student in Los Angeles, California. She loves spending her summers at camp on the East Coast. During the school year, she enjoys rowing, soccer, cooking, basketball, preparing cheese plates, and playing with her dachshund, Nathan.

Notes

Notes

Notes

Notes

Notes